THE ROWERS' CODE

7 Principles to Power-Up Your Life and Your Team

Marilyn Krichko
with Jane Rollinson
Authors of *The Rowers' Code:*
A Business Parable of How to
Pull Together as a Team - and Win!

PARTICIPANT WORKBOOK

Contact Information:

Criterion Consulting Solutions LLC
PO Box 99613
Seattle, WA 98139

1-855-ROW-CODE
www.rowerscode.com

For bulk purchases of this book in the U.S. please contact 855-ROW-CODE.

HIGHPOINT EXECUTIVE PUBLISHING www.highpointpubs.com

Table of Contents

Teamwork Starts with You!

What if everyone on your team worked in perfect sync? What would that look like?

What if you loved going to work in the morning? How would it feel?

What if you were not afraid of having honest conversations with your colleagues and your boss? How would it change things?

Teamwork is the heartbeat of every successful organization. Yet, so many teams are dysfunctional. The purpose of this workbook is to help you discover successful teambuilding and communication principles, and then apply them to your own life so that you work better with those around you. It's as simple as that.

There are two things you need to know to get started:

1. TEAMWORK MATTERS!

2. TEAMWORK STARTS WITH YOU!

Although "team" implies the joint effort of many people, in reality you cannot control what other people do. You can only control what *you* do.

Here's what you will do during this workshop:

1. LEARN The Rowers' Code and other positive team building and communication principles that are memorable and easy to understand.
2. PERSONALIZE what you learn so it has meaning to you.
3. APPLY what you have personalized to your everyday life.
4. COMMIT to positive behavior, resulting in new positive habits. Over time, your positive habits will help build a culture of excellence.

I invite you to get in the boat with me and experience The Rowers' Code principles first hand as you apply them to your own life and your team!

Workshop Objectives

All too often, people leave teambuilding workshops and retreats without being able to make a connection between the activities they did at the event, and their everyday work. The result is minimal positive impact, and sometimes even negative impact.

This workbook and the exercises inside are designed to help you make that very important connection, so that you get the most out of your interactions with others – and they get the most out of their interactions with you.

What do you want to get out of this workshop?

_____

_____

_____

_____

_____

_____

_____

_____

_____

_____

ROWING – Experience the Power!

There is nothing like being part of a team that is aligned and working together in perfect synchronicity.

Why rowing? What does rowing have to do with teambuilding? Why is rowing the ultimate team sport?

A sweep boat, called an "eight," holds eight rowers and someone to steer called a coxswain. The boats are 60 feet long and weigh about 235 pounds. It doesn't matter who you are - you could be the strongest person in the world and you wouldn't be able to get one of the sweep boats out of the boathouse and on the water without a team and a team effort. So, from the very start, rowing is about **TEAMWORK!**

Teamwork is a choice. Being a team player is not for everyone, just like rowing is not for everyone. You can stand on the dock and watch as the boat rows away. You can wave at your team, cheer for them, or pass out drinks when they are thirsty. However, unless you get in the boat yourself, you'll never know what it really feels like to own your seat and own your oar, helping to power up the boat. There is nothing like it.

Rowing is certainly NOT for faint of heart because it takes determination, discipline and focus. Traits most dedicated rowers have are:

- Commitment to putting the team first
- Respectful
- Responsible
- Focused
- Determined
- Disciplined
- Aware of the big picture and their part in it

- Aware of others
- Trustworthy
- Honest
- Ethical
- Hard working
- Punctual

You might think, "Wow, that is some list." Yes, it is. You might be able to row a boat without some of those traits, but there is one trait that you must have to row a sweep boat – a commitment to putting the team first.

Sweep boats are designed for speed. It takes the right combination of people in the right seats to make the boat go fast. Every rower in an eight can row in any seat. *The challenge is to be in the seat that maximizes the strengths of the entire team, even as your team changes and as you get into new or different boats.*

You are probably starting to draw parallels between rowing and work as your read this. It's what I did years ago as I sat in a sweep boat seat in Philadelphia, and it's why I developed teambuilding programs using rowing in the first place. Rowing is a team effort; work is a team effort. Rowing seeks to maximize individual skills in a team setting – we do the same thing at work.

Everyone can picture a boat where everyone is rowing well together and everyone can picture one that is not. When I ask teams to draw pictures of their current state at work using boats, they can easily draw what that looks like. They can also easily draw what they want their ideal state to look like. Team members sometimes draw empty seats in a boat showing they need either a skill or a person filling a role or providing something their team doesn't currently have.

But, drawing and making change happen are two different things. This is where rowing plays a key role. Rowing helps you *become* the change you envision and experience what it feels like, and with instant feedback. It lets each person understand and experience that **EVERYTHING YOU DO AND DON'T DO AFFECTS OTHERS!** Rowing is exciting, fun and memorable!

Learning how to row together as a team is an experience that literally puts everyone in the same boat. It's a type of team bonding that instills trust because you have to rely on your team members to do their part. You cannot power up the boat yourself, no matter how hard you try.

What is the Rowers' Code?

The Rowers' Code is a simple, actionable set of principles that can be applied to every workplace and team scenario to supercharge performance! It's not important what The Rowers' Code means to me. What it means to you and how you apply it in your own team is what matters!

Are you up to the Challenge?

The Rowers' Code Introduction

Rowers' Code Principle	Explanation	Things to Think About
#1 Always Do What's Best for the Team	Putting the interests of your team in front of your own. Rowing as "one boat" instead of everyone rowing in their own direction.	What can I do to row as "one boat"?
#2 Give Every Seat Equal Value	Treating others with respect, acknowledging and trusting in each other's strengths.	Do each person's strengths align with the seats in the boat?
#3 Carry Your Load	Knowing and doing your share of what needs to be done.	Do I know what I need to do to carry my load?
#4 Balance the Boat	Attaining the right mix.	Do we have the right mix to attain balance?
#5 Stay in Sync	Timing is everything. Realizing that what you do or don't do affects others.	What can I do to stay in sync with my team?
#6 Lead By Example	Trusting in yourself and others, sharing leadership responsibility.	Where are the leadership opportunities as I learn to row? If I want to lead, am I in a leadership seat?
#7 Keep Everything in the Boat	Clear and honest communication with your teammates.	Is there anything I need to talk to the team about before we start rowing?

ROWING – Experience the Power!

Notes on The Rowers' Code

_____

_____

_____

_____

_____

Which Rowers' Code principle stands out the most for you when you think of the rowing challenge ahead?

_____

_____

Why?

_____

_____

_____

_____

_____

_____

Tools & Resources

Boat

- 60 feet long
- Weighs approximately 235 pounds
- 9 seats
- Foot stretcher with shoes
- Rigger to hold oars
- Sliding seat

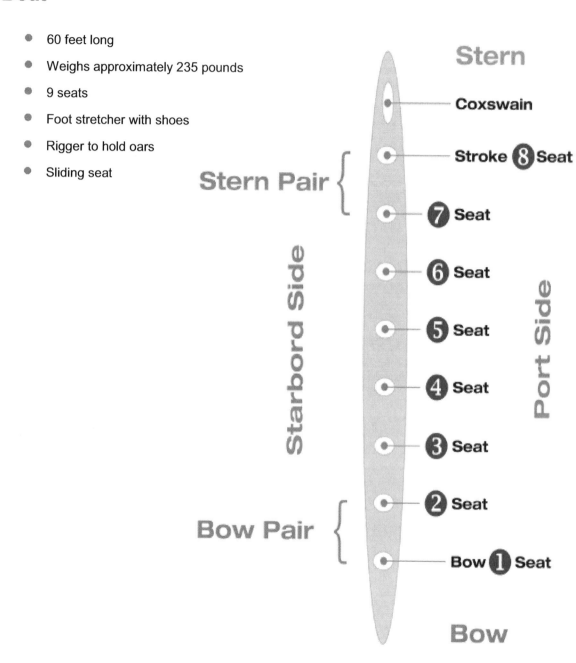

Oars

- Approximately 14' long
- The boat is propelled forward with the oars
- Oars help balance and stabilize the boat

Coach

- Sees the big picture and gets everyone focused on the common goal
- Motivates and teaches individuals while facilitating teamwork

Crew

- 9 members – 8 rowers and one coxswain
- Each person has a specific role; all are equally important

Things to Consider

Synchronization – ability to move in concert with others, such as your rowing teammates
Pace – ability to keep up a constant rate of progress, such as a rowing stroke
Balance – ability to hold calm and steady, such as keeping the boat stable
Focus – ability to concentrate on an action or objective, such as the movements of the rowing stroke
Leadership –ability to provide direction and guidance, such as providing an example to those behind you in the boat
Skill – ability to perform something competently, such as rowing

Exercise 1 On the first line, write your name and give yourself a ranking based on the scale:

0 = Couch potato, 5 = Olympic rower

Name	Synchronization	Pace	Balance	Focus	Leadership	Skill

Exercise 2 Write your teammate's names and the ranking they gave themselves. Use this chart to help with the next exercise.

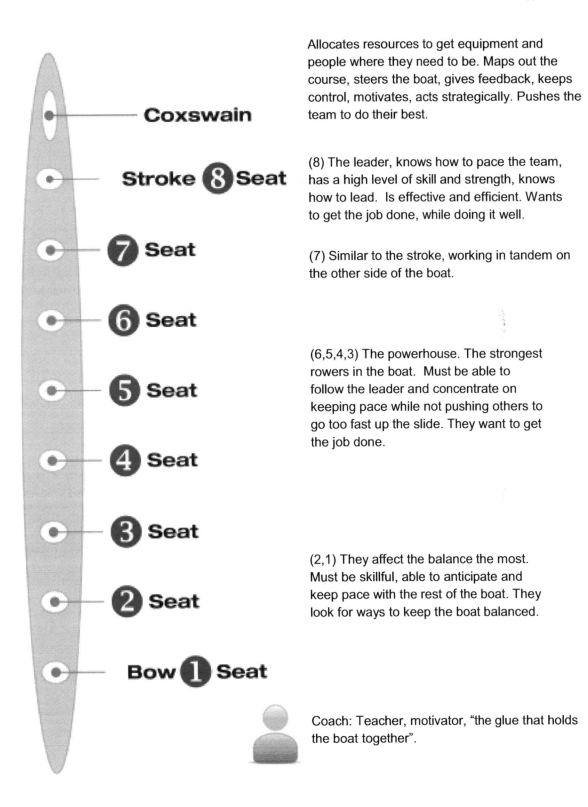

Coxswain

Allocates resources to get equipment and people where they need to be. Maps out the course, steers the boat, gives feedback, keeps control, motivates, acts strategically. Pushes the team to do their best.

Stroke 8 Seat

(8) The leader, knows how to pace the team, has a high level of skill and strength, knows how to lead. Is effective and efficient. Wants to get the job done, while doing it well.

7 Seat

(7) Similar to the stroke, working in tandem on the other side of the boat.

6 Seat

5 Seat

(6,5,4,3) The powerhouse. The strongest rowers in the boat. Must be able to follow the leader and concentrate on keeping pace while not pushing others to go too fast up the slide. They want to get the job done.

4 Seat

3 Seat

2 Seat

(2,1) They affect the balance the most. Must be skillful, able to anticipate and keep pace with the rest of the boat. They look for ways to keep the boat balanced.

Bow 1 Seat

Coach: Teacher, motivator, "the glue that holds the boat together".

Team Roles & Setting Your Boat

Exercise 3 Using the descriptions from the previous page and the information about team strengths, determine who will fill each seat in your boat to maximize performance. Record this information below.

Coxswain _____

Stroke **8** Seat _____

7 Seat _____

6 Seat _____

5 Seat _____

4 Seat _____

3 Seat _____

2 Seat _____

Bow **1** Seat _____

Did you end up in the seat that you thought was the best fit for you and for the team? Why or why not?

_____

_____

_____

Do you feel that the seats people are in will maximize the strengths of the entire team? Why or why not?

_____

_____

_____

What challenges did you face as a team picking seats that maximized the strengths of each person on the team?

_____

_____

_____

What did you learn about yourself and your teammates during this exercise?

_____

_____

_____

Team Language

Back - Push the oar through the water to move the boat sternward.

Blades feathered - Blades parallel to the water

Blades square - Blades squared (perpendicular) to the water

Catch - The starting point in the stroke when the blade enters the water

Drive - The midpoint of the stroke when the blade is in the water and you push your legs down

Finish - The end of the stroke, when the blade is released from the water

Hold water - Press the flat of blade on the water to stop the boat.

Set the boat - Use hand heights to balance the boat.

Way enough - Stop what you are doing.

Our Boat

Exercise 4 Pick a name for your team boat

_____

Rowing Debrief

What went well?

_____

_____

_____

What didn't go well?

_____

_____

_____

If you did this exercise again, what would you change?

_____

_____

_____

What did you learn about yourself?

_____

_____

_____

What did you learn about your teammates?

_____

_____

Rowing Debrief

What was your biggest challenge?

_____

_____

_____

What was easy for you?

_____

_____

_____

Were you able to use your strengths in a team setting? Why or why not?

_____

_____

_____

What parallels can you draw between rowing and work?

_____

_____

_____

The Rowers' Code Summary

Rowers' Code Principle	Explanation	Attribute
#1 Always Do What's Best for the Team	Putting the interests of your team in front of your own. Rowing as "one boat" instead of everyone rowing in their own direction.	Commitment
#2 Give Every Seat Equal Value	Treating others with respect, acknowledging and trusting in each other's strengths.	Acknowledgment
#3 Carry Your Load	Knowing and doing your share of what needs to be done.	Responsibility and Accountability
#4 Balance the Boat	Attaining the right mix.	Organizational and Self-Awareness
#5 Stay in Sync	Timing is everything. Realizing that what you do or don't do affects others.	Situational Awareness
#6 Lead By Example	Trusting in yourself and others, sharing leadership responsibility.	Trust
#7 Keep Everything in the Boat	Clear and honest communication with your teammates.	Integrity and Ownership

Notes on The Rowers' Code

_____

_____

_____

_____

_____

Which Rowers' Code principle stands out the most for you when you think of the challenges ahead?

_____

_____

Why?

_____

_____

_____

_____

_____

Draw a picture using a boat or boats that shows the current state of your team.

The Model We Will Use

<table>
<tr><td>**LEARN**</td><td>To gain knowledge or understanding of The Rowers' Code and other teambuilding and communication core principles.</td><td>**PERSONALIZE**</td><td>To make the connection between the things you learn and your own situation.</td><td>**APPLY**</td><td>To put the things you learn into action.</td><td>**COMMIT**</td><td>To carry into action daily, forming habits, eventually building a culture of excellence.</td></tr>
</table>

PRINCIPLE #1
Always Do What's Best for the Team

Always doing what's best for the team involves a commitment to putting the team first. In rowing terms it means a commitment to rowing as "one boat" instead of doing your own thing and rowing in your own direction.

Patrick Lencioni could not have said it any better…

"If you could get all the people in an organization rowing in the same direction, you could dominate any industry, in any market, against any competition, at any time."

From *The Five Dysfunctions of a Team*
By Patrick Lencioni

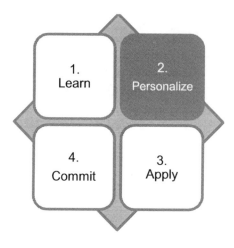

The word "commitment" implies some sort of agreement to do something. In the case of a team commitment, it's to take some expected action that positively impacts the team and adds value to the team effort.

What does "putting the team first" mean to you?

_____

_____

_____

_____

_____

What are the challenges of putting the team first?

_____

_____

_____

_____

List positive and negative behaviors below that show either commitment or lack of commitment to putting the team first.

#1 Always Do What's Best for the Team

Positive (+) behaviors showing commitment to putting the team first	Negative (-) behaviors showing lack of commitment to putting the team first
•	•
•	•
•	•
•	•
•	•
•	•

Pick 5 of the positive behaviors, list them in the table below and rate yourself.

Behavior	Strongly Agree (6)	Agree (5)	Slightly Agree (4)	Slightly Disagree (3)	Disagree (2)	Strongly Disagree (1)

What stops you from putting your team first?

_____

_____

_____

What can you do to overcome these obstacles?

_____

_____

_____

_____

_____

#1 Always Do What's Best for the Team

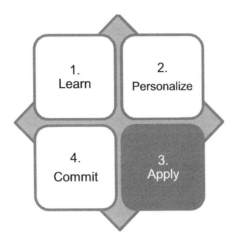

In order for the team to be successful, which team projects or decisions are the most important to complete over the next three (3) months?

-
-
-

List the project or decision along with what the team agreed on.

Project or Decision	What the Team Agreed On
• • •	
• • •	
• • •	

Circle items the team agreed on where you should take some action.

To what extent do team members put the interests of the team first?

1 = Not at all   10 = Always

1	2	3	4	5	6	7	8	9	10

For each team item you circled where you should take some action, list your commitments (next steps) and how you will measure your success.

Project/Decision Name	Team agreements involving me	My commitments (next steps)	My measure of success
	• • •		
	• • •		
	• • •		

#1 Always Do What's Best for the Team

List obstacles that might stop you from honoring your commitments.

_____

_____

_____

_____

_____

What are you planning on doing to make sure you are successful?

_____

_____

_____

_____

_____

How will you report your progress back to the team?

_____

_____

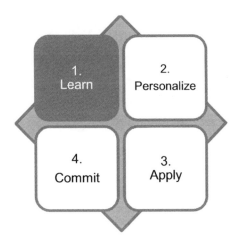

PRINCIPLE #2
Give Every Seat Equal Value

The way in which we value ourselves and others can determine our survival in a competitive and changing environment.

There are three ways in which people know that you value them:

1. You **listen** to them.
2. You **ask** for their opinions.
3. You **include** them in decision making.

Life is complex, at times you may think one role is more important than another, but at the end of the day it is the effort of everyone that will give your team the big wins.

It starts with valuing the usefulness of everyone and expecting the best from them.

The first step to valuing others is to merely give others a chance. Listen to each other, encourage each other and it will pay off. Instead of checking out, people will start to engage more with you. You might be pleasantly surprised at the result.

The other side of the value coin involves value you bring to your team. Gaining value is not always easy, and people's strengths are not always apparent.

The key to valuing others and being valued by others is an understanding that doing great things takes a team effort. Simply put, we need each other. The best teams are made up of diverse individuals with a variety of backgrounds, interests and capabilities. Learning how to work together requires a commitment to discovering how team members can leverage their diverse talents.

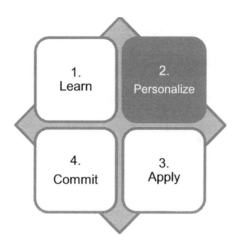

"Acknowledgement" means to take notice in a favorable way. It's a key part of assigning value to someone or something.

What does "give every seat equal value" mean to you?

_____

_____

_____

_____

What are the challenges of giving every seat equal value?

_____

_____

_____

_____

List positive and negative behaviors below that show others are equally valued or that others are NOT equally valued.

#2 Give Every Seat Equal Value

Positive (+) behaviors that show others are equally valued

-
-
-
-
-
-

Negative (-) behaviors that show others are not equally valued

-
-
-
-
-
-

Pick 5 of the positive behaviors, list them in the table below and rate yourself.

Behavior	Strongly Agree (6)	Agree (5)	Slightly Agree (4)	Slightly Disagree (3)	Disagree (2)	Strongly Disagree (1)

Using the table below, list your responses to the following questions for yourself and your team members:

1. What role does each person have on the team?
2. How long has each person been on the team?
3. What 2-3 strengths does each person bring to the team?
4. What one area for improvement could add value to the team?

List your name first, and then your teammates' names.

Name	Role	Time on team	2-3 Strengths	Area for Improvement

#2 Give Every Seat Equal Value

Adding value and getting feedback go hand-in-hand. Ask your peers what they identified as your strengths and your areas for improvement.

My Strengths	My Areas for Improvement
• • •	•
• • •	•
• • •	•
• • •	•
• • •	•
• • •	•
• • •	•
• • •	•

Peer Feedback

Which strengths do you agree with?

_____

_____

_____

_____

Which strengths do you disagree with, if any, and why?

_____

_____

_____

_____

Which areas for improvement do you agree with?

_____

_____

_____

_____

#2 Give Every Seat Equal Value

Which areas for improvement do you disagree with? Why?

_____

_____

_____

_____

List anything stopping you from applying your strengths:

_____

_____

_____

_____

List anything you do that stops others from being able to use their strengths:

_____

_____

_____

_____

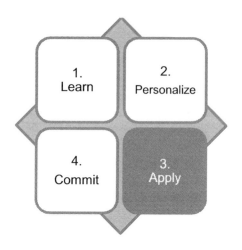

TAPPING INTO YOUR STRENGTHS

List your top three strengths and ways you could use them to help the team succeed:

Strength	Application or Project

#2 Give Every Seat Equal Value

List one area for personal improvement, which if changed, could have a major impact on the team. How will it have a positive impact?

_____

_____

_____

_____

_____

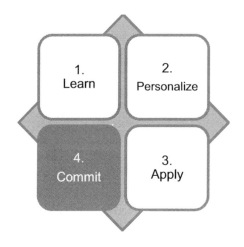

How often do team members use one another's strengths?

1 = Never   10 = All the time

1	2	3	4	5	6	7	8	9	10

List your commitment to next steps below and your measure of success:

Strength	Application or Project	My Next Steps	How I Will Know I am Successful
Area for improvement	**Application or Project**	**My Next Steps**	**How I Will Know I am Successful**

List any obstacles that might stop you from using your strengths or working on your area for improvement.

_____

_____

_____

_____

TAPPING INTO THE STRENGTHS OF YOUR PEERS

Pick one other person on your team and list how you can help them apply their strengths to one project you are working on together where they are already not using that strength and how you can help them with their area for improvement. Also, list what you expect to get out of your effort. Set up a meeting with your peer to discuss an action plan for moving forward. Plan your plan, work your plan.

Peer Name: _____

Date for initial meeting: _____

Peer Strength	Application or Project	My Next Steps to help my teammate use their strength	What I expect from my effort
Peer Area for Improvement	**Application or Project**	**My Next Steps to help my teammate with their area for improvement**	**What I expect from my effort**

Helping Others

Meeting notes from initial meeting.

_____

_____

_____

_____

What went well?

_____

_____

_____

What didn't go well?

_____

_____

_____

Were you able to help your peer? Why or why not?

_____

_____

_____

_____

#2 Give Every Seat Equal Value

Date for follow-up meeting: _____

Meeting notes from follow up meeting.

_____

_____

_____

_____

What went well?

_____

_____

_____

What didn't go well?

_____

_____

_____

Were you able to help your peer? Why or why not?

_____

_____

_____

_____

List lessons learned from this experience.

_____

_____

_____

_____

If you repeated this exercise, what would you change?

_____

_____

_____

_____

Getting Help from a Peer

Peer Name: _____

Date for initial meeting: _____

Meeting notes from initial meeting.

_____

_____

_____

_____

What went well?

_____

_____

_____

What didn't go well?

_____

_____

_____

Were you able to get help from your peer? Why or why not?

_____

_____

_____

Date for follow-up meeting: _____

Meeting notes from follow up meeting.

_____

_____

_____

_____

What went well?

_____

_____

_____

What didn't go well?

_____

_____

_____

#2 Give Every Seat Equal Value

Were you able to get help from your peer? Why or why not?

_____

_____

_____

List lessons learned from this experience.

_____

_____

_____

_____

If you repeated this exercise, what would you change?

_____

_____

_____

_____

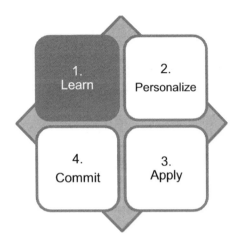

PRINCIPLE #3
Carry Your Load

In a competitive rowing boat, there is nothing like the moment when each person is pulling his or her own weight and the boat starts to lift off the water. It starts to soar, barely touching the surface, and everyone in the boat feels like a champion.

"Carrying your load" requires responsibility to the team. Not just general responsibility – that's far too vague and far too easy to get off track without even knowing it.

The key to successful responsibility is **accountability**. Accountability involves a focus on doing the right things right.

Although there is no magic formula for measuring success, there are a few simple rules you can follow.

Ask yourself and others...

- Am I measuring the right things?

- Will my measurement verify I am focusing on the right things?

- Is my measurement good enough to base decisions on?

- Will my measurement give me an accurate picture of reality?

- Will my measurement let me know if I need to correct a problem, or remove an obstacle?

- Will my measurement help me prioritize my efforts?

- Will my measurement show I have improved, slipped, or stayed on track?

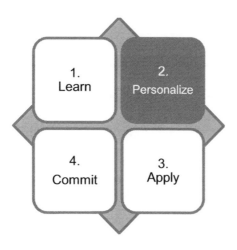

What does "carry your load" mean to you?

_____

_____

_____

_____

_____

What are the challenges of carrying your load?

_____

_____

_____

_____

_____

_____

What does being "responsible" mean to you?

_____

_____

_____

_____

_____

What does being "accountable" mean to you?

_____

_____

_____

_____

_____

What is the difference between responsibility and accountability?

_____

_____

_____

_____

_____

List positive and negative behaviors below that show responsibility and accountability or lack of responsibility and lack of accountability.

#3 Carry Your Load

Positive (+) behaviors showing responsibility and accountability

-
-
-
-
-
-

Negative (-) behaviors showing lack of responsibility and lack of accountability

-
-
-
-
-
-

Pick 5 of the positive behaviors, list them in the table below and rate yourself.

Behavior	Strongly Agree (6)	Agree (5)	Slightly Agree (4)	Slightly Disagree (3)	Disagree (2)	Strongly Disagree (1)

How do you hold each other on your team accountable?

_____

_____

_____

_____

_____

When goals slip, what do you do to get back on track?

_____

_____

_____

_____

_____

When you meet your goals, what do you do to acknowledge your success?

_____

_____

_____

_____

_____

#3 Carry Your Load

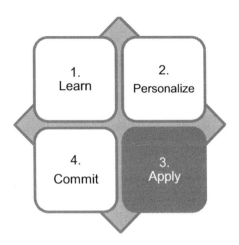

List your primary areas of responsibility and your measure(s) of success in the table below:

Area(s) of Responsibility	Measure(s) of Success
• • •	• • •
• • •	• • •
• • •	• • •

Compare your measures of success to the "simple rules" below and make adjustments as necessary.

- Am I measuring the right things?

- Will my measurement verify I am focusing on the right things?

- Is my measurement good enough to base decisions on?

- Will my measurement give me an accurate picture of reality?

- Will my measurement let me know if I need to correct a problem, or remove an obstacle?

- Will my measurement help me prioritize my efforts?

- Will my measurement show I have improved, slipped, or stayed on track?

#3 Carry Your Load

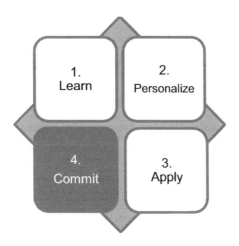

To what extent are team members held accountable for carrying their load?

1 = Not at all   10 = To the maximum

1	2	3	4	5	6	7	8	9	10

Use the following Progress Board to map your progress. Record the key responsibilities and measures to which you are committed.

Update the board each week to show your progress. Circle your successes and add them to your team success board.

My Progress

Responsibility	Measure(s) of Success	Outcome Week 1	Outcome Week2	Outcome Week 3

Team Success Board

Week 1	Week 2	Week 3
•	•	•
•	•	•
•	•	•
•	•	•
•	•	•
•	•	•

PRINCIPLE #4
Balance the Boat

How balanced is your life?

It's a simple question with the probability of a complex answer. Attaining balance is one of the things we first learn how to do. It is also one of the things most people struggle with their entire lives. As we strive to make it through the day, things get out of balance. *A great skill to have is knowing when things are off kilter and how to get them back in alignment quickly.*

Don't be afraid to "rock the boat". Sometimes, rocking the boat is a good way to know where you really are and, if off balance, it can help you get right back in balance as a team.

Everything you do, and don't do, affects others.

Team balance has to do with awareness of the big picture and your role in it. Attaining the right mix of people, skills and experience on your team is vital. The right mix helps you avoid being one sided and helps maintain a healthy balance during challenging times.

Ask yourself and your team:

1. Do we have the right mix of people on our team?
2. Are our workloads reasonable?
3. Is each person in the right role?
4. Do we understand the objectives of the organization and our team?
5. Does everyone actively participate in decision making?
6. Do we have adequate time to complete our work?
7. Does each person understand what they are required to do for the team to be successful?
8. What does having a balanced team feel like?

Where does balance start? As with most things, balance starts with you!

#4 Balance the Boat

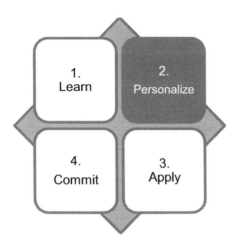

How do you know when your life is in or out of balance?

_____

_____

_____

What do you do to stay balanced and avoid getting out of balance?

_____

_____

_____

When things get out of balance in your life, what do you do to get back in balance?

_____

_____

_____

List positive and negative behaviors below that show either organizational and self-awareness and lack of organizational and self-awareness.

#4 Balance the Boat

Positive (+) behaviors showing organizational and self-awareness
-
-
-
-
-
-

Negative (-) behaviors showing lack of organizational and self-awareness
-
-
-
-
-
-

Pick 5 of the positive behaviors, list them in the table below and rate yourself.

Behavior	Strongly Agree (6)	Agree (5)	Slightly Agree (4)	Slightly Disagree (3)	Disagree (2)	Strongly Disagree (1)

#4 Balance the Boat

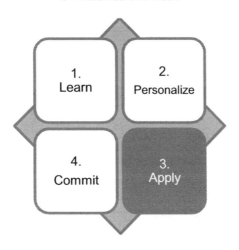

How do you know when your team is in-balance, or off-balance?

_____

_____

_____

_____

What balance issues or challenges does your team face? What are the contributing factors?

Issue(s)	Contributing Factor(s)

What behaviors help your team attain and maintain balance?

_____

_____

_____

_____

How balanced is your work life?

1 = Completely out of balance   10 = Perfectly balanced

1	2	3	4	5	6	7	8	9	10

List positive behaviors that help you keep your work life balanced.

- _____

- _____

- _____

#4 Balance the Boat

How balanced is your team "boat"?

1 = Completely out of balance   10 = Perfectly balanced

1	2	3	4	5	6	7	8	9	10

List negative behaviors that stop you from attaining and maintaining balance on your team.

- _____

- _____

- _____

List behaviors are you willing to commit to over the next 3 weeks:

Positive Behaviors I Will Start Doing	**Negative behaviors I Will Stop Doing…**
•	•
•	•
•	•
•	•

When things get out of balance, what strategies will you use to get back to a place of balance?

_____

_____

_____

_____

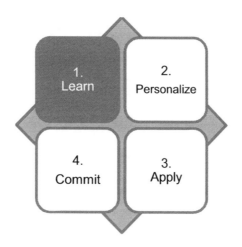

PRINCIPLE #5
Stay in Sync

When we are in perfect sync it feels like everything is right with the world. When we are not in sync with those around us, we wonder, "what happened?"

On some days my sister and I try phoning each other cross-country and cannot seem to connect. We say our "tele-rhythms" are off. Other days we both pick up the phone to call – and before the phone even rings – we realize we were both dialing at exactly the same time. Now that's being in sync!

Being in sync requires an understanding of where people around you are at a certain point in time – it is situational awareness.

Have you ever spoken to co-workers and realized part of the way through that they were not listening? Maybe they didn't have any bandwidth. Maybe they were distracted. There are plenty of distractions today trying to get us to multi-task, and there are plenty of studies proving why we shouldn't.

Focusing on positive behavior helps everyone.   Let people know when it's a good time to talk and engage in decision making, but also let them know when you don't have enough bandwidth to engage.

This section is designed to help you identify:

- What helps keeps you in sync
- What gets you out of sync
- How to quickly get back in sync when things are off kilter

What does being "in sync" mean to you?

_____

_____

_____

_____

Do you know when you are in sync with others? How? Give examples:

_____

_____

_____

_____

How do you know when you are out of sync with others? Give examples:

_____

_____

_____

_____

List positive and negative behaviors below showing either situational awareness and staying in sync or lack of situational awareness and being out of sync.

#5 Stay in Sync

Positive (+) behaviors showing situational awareness and staying in sync

-
-
-
-
-

Negative (-) behaviors showing lack of situational awareness and being out of sync

-
-
-
-
-

Pick 5 of the positive behaviors, list them in the table below and rate yourself.

Behavior	Strongly Agree (6)	Agree (5)	Slightly Agree (4)	Slightly Disagree (3)	Disagree (2)	Strongly Disagree (1)

Is there anything stopping you from being in sync with your teammates?

_____

_____

_____

_____

_____

_____

Is there anything stopping your team members from being in sync with you?

_____

_____

_____

_____

_____

_____

#5 Stay in Sync

In order for your team to be in perfect synchronicity, list three positive behaviors that <u>you</u> would like to start doing at work:

1. _____

2.
   _____

3. _____

In order for your team to be in perfect synchronicity, list negative behaviors that <u>you</u> would like to stop doing at work:

-

-

-

Circle one positive and one negative item above, which you feel would have the most impact on your team.

In order for your team to be in perfect synchronicity, list three positive behaviors you would like to see team members doing at work.

1. _____

2. _____

3. _____

In order for your team to be in perfect synchronicity, list negative behaviors you would like to see team members stop doing at work:

-

-

-

Circle one positive and one negative item above, which you feel would have the most impact on your team.

#5 Stay in Sync

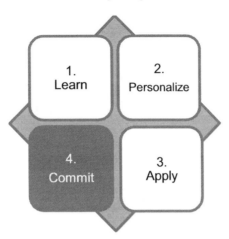

How in sync is your team right now?

1 = Completely out of sync   10 = Perfectly in sync

1	2	3	4	5	6	7	8	9	10

If you are not a "10", brainstorm ideas with your teammates to quickly close the gap. What ideas did you come up with?

-
-
-
-
-

Which ideas do you feel will have the most positive impact on team synchronicity?

_____

_____

List actions you are willing to commit to keep your own work life in sync.

Positive Behaviors I Will Start Doing	Negative behaviors I Will Stop Doing
•	•
•	•
•	•
•	•

PRINCIPLE #6
Lead by Example

Why should you lead by example? Because people don't follow words, people follow people. We've all heard the sayings "talk is cheap" and "action speaks louder than words." Both sayings are especially true when it comes to leadership. Leading by example can be difficult at times because it requires us to step up and hold ourselves to a higher standard.

I can tell you this about higher standards - they pay off! When we lead by example, we have something to be proud of at the end of the day that no one can take away.

It takes belief in yourself and others and trust to share in leadership responsibility. Trust turns "passive" into "active." Instead of just waving from the dock, trust helps us get in the boat and start rowing!

Leading by example is for everyone. It's not just for the CEO, the manager or the boss. There are many opportunities to lead in small and big ways every day. Look around you. I am sure, if you try, you can find all kinds of opportunity to lead. The first step is to trust in yourself and give it a try.

Ask yourself: What can I do today that someone else would want to follow?

Do what you say you will do, tackle one issue at a time, and constantly lift the bar.

#6 Lead by Example

I remember my first big chance at being a leader. I was terrified! When I confided in my boss and told him how scared I was, he responded by saying, "It's ok, we will help you." His words of support gave me the confidence I needed to give it a try.

Then, when I did make mistakes, my team had my back, instead of throwing me under the bus! Their behavior, when I fell short, was such a great example and helped give me the confidence I needed to carry on. I'm happy to say that I have had many great leaders in my life who have shown me the way through their own example – people I can look up to and go to for advice.

I encourage you to search for people you can look up to and go to for advice – people who set an excellent example and have leadership qualities you respect.

Be the best you can be every day because there is someone, somewhere, who might need direction and a great leadership example to follow. That leader could be you!

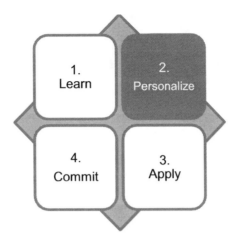

What does "Lead by Example" mean to you?

_____

_____

_____

Name a leader whom you trust.

_____

What did they do to earn your trust?

_____

_____

_____

What leadership traits do you admire in them?

_____

List positive and negative behaviors below that show leading by example or a lack of leading by example.

#6 Lead By Example

Positive (+) behaviors showing leading by example	Negative (-) behaviors showing a lack of leading by example
•	•
•	•
•	•
•	•
•	•
•	•

Pick 5 of the positive behaviors, list them in the table below and rate yourself.

Behavior	Strongly Agree (6)	Agree (5)	Slightly Agree (4)	Slightly Disagree (3)	Disagree (2)	Strongly Disagree (1)

Which situations bring out the leader in you? Why?

_____

_____

_____

_____

In which situations have you avoided taking a leadership role? Why?

_____

_____

_____

_____

When do you excel as a leader?

_____

_____

_____

_____

When do you fall short as a leader?

_____

_____

_____

_____

#6 Lead by Example

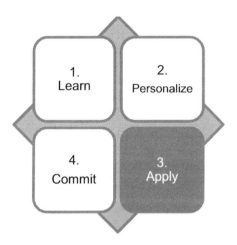

Identify some opportunities at work where you could step up and take more of a leadership role.

-

-

-

 List the opportunities below, action you could take, and how you will know you are successful.

Opportunity	Action	Measure of success

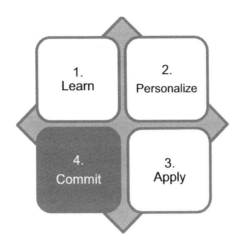

How much do you trust in others to lead?

1 = I do not trust in others to lead   10 = I completely trust in others to lead

1	2	3	4	5	6	7	8	9	10

How much do you trust in yourself to lead?

1 = I do not trust in myself to lead   10 = I completely trust in myself to lead

1	2	3	4	5	6	7	8	9	10

Pick one leadership opportunity and describe it below. Pick an accountability partner you can go to for advice and direction. Set a date for a meeting with him or her and take some notes regarding the advice you get.

Leadership Opportunity _____

Accountability partner name _____

Notes from initial accountability partner meeting:

_____

_____

_____

#6 Lead by Example

The outcome of the meeting with your accountability partner should be to verify that the leadership role you want to take is appropriate for you and that your next steps make sense and are likely produce a successful result. Follow up with your accountability partner weekly to get advice and direction.

Week 1 Activities/next Steps	Effects of Activities
•	•
•	•
•	•

Notes from 2nd accountability partner meeting:

What went well?

What didn't go well?

What you would like to change:

Week 2 Activities	Effects of Activities
•	•
•	•
•	•

Notes from 3rd accountability partner meeting:

What went well?

What didn't go well?

What you would like to change:

Week 3 Activities	Effects of Activities
•	•
•	•
•	•

Notes from final accountability partner meeting:

What went well?

What didn't go well?

What you would like to change:

Were your meetings with your accountability partner worthwhile? Why or why not?

_____

_____

_____

Did you attain the results you expected from your effort? Why or why not?

_____

_____

_____

What did you learn from this experience?

_____

_____

_____

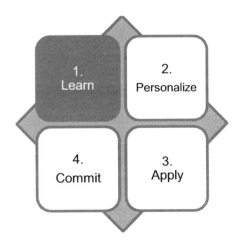

PRINCIPLE #7
Keep Everything in the Boat

Talking outside the team is the #1 killer of teams!

Talking outside the team breaks down trust and destroys relationships and careers. So, why do people do it? Usually because they feel they have no one on the team to talk to. Or people believe the environment on their team isn't safe enough to bring up issues and work through them.

Creating a culture of teamwork requires every person to own the way they communicate with each other. It requires integrity. Having open and honest conversations is the starting point.

You might feel like you are rocking the boat at times, but isn't that how you will also find out what you and your team are made of? If you bury things under the rug, they will just fester anyhow. Honest and respectful communication builds trust and forms solid relationships.

A few good rules for open and honest communication are:

- Listen with an open mind and open ears.
- Ask clarifying questions if you don't understand.
- Hear each other out.
- Stick to the real issues.
- Bring help in if you're getting nowhere (be careful who you bring in – not all advice is good advice).

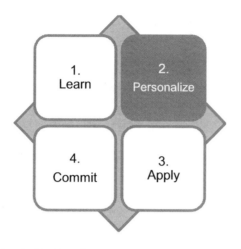

What does "keep everything in the boat" mean to you?

_____

_____

_____

_____

Is this an area that is easy for you, or difficult for you? Why?

_____

_____

_____

What benefits are there to addressing issues with your teammates?

_____

_____

_____

_____

What downsides are there to addressing issues with your teammates?

_____

_____

_____

_____

List positive and negative behaviors below that show integrity and ownership for issues or a lack of integrity and ownership for issues.

#7 Keep Everything in the Boat

Positive (+) behaviors showing integrity and ownership for issues

-
-
-
-
-

Negative (-) behaviors showing lack of integrity and ownership for issues

-
-
-
-
-

Pick 5 of the positive behaviors, list them in the table below and rate yourself.

Behavior	Strongly Agree (6)	Agree (5)	Slightly Agree (4)	Slightly Disagree (3)	Disagree (2)	Strongly Disagree (1)

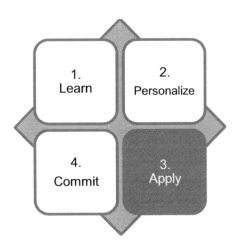

List any issues blocking your team from being successful.

_____

_____

_____

_____

List how have you tried to address these issues.

Issue	Actions to Date

How do issues on your team get identified and resolved?

_____

_____

_____

Is this a positive experience or a negative one? Why?

_____

_____

_____

What challenges do you face when trying to bring up issues with your teammates?

_____

_____

_____

What stops you from bringing up issues?

_____

_____

_____

#7 Keep Everything in the Boat

What would make it easier for you to bring up issues with your teammates?

_____

_____

_____

How can you make it easier for others to bring up issues with you?

_____

_____

_____

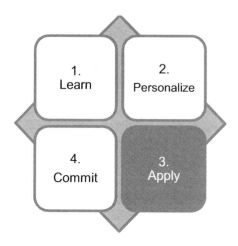

List an issue you would like to openly discuss with your team. Frame it up for discussion using the framework below:

Issue	
Why is it important to you?	
Who should participate in the discussion?	
What do you want from your teammates? (Input? Help making a decision? Help removing an obstacle? Other?)	
How much time do you need to discuss it?	
List additional concerns, or other notes.	

How good are you at working out issues directly with your teammates.

1 = Very bad   10 = Excellent

1	2	3	4	5	6	7	8	9	10

Using the discussion framework from the previous page, frame up any issues you have, and schedule a meeting with your team for discussion

Date of meeting	
Issue	
What went well?	
What didn't go well?	
Outcome	
Next steps	

What will you do differently the next time you have an issue to bring up?

_____

_____

_____

_____

The Challenge

It was a bit late to be getting out on the water. I should have been at the boathouse by 5 a.m. and on the water by 5:15 to beat the power boat traffic. But, I woke up late that day and I wasn't so excited about going out in my single shell. The year before, I had cracked my kneecap when I slipped on a wet leaf on my way to pick up an extension cord for my father-in-laws 80th birthday. The rehab was extensive. I hadn't rowed for what felt like forever. Instead I spent that summer, the next fall and winter biking on my indoor bike in the basement. It was nothing like rowing.

Spring came around and my rowing doubles partner finally got me to agree to get into a boat with her several times. Feeling confident again, on May 25, I rowed away from the dock in my Hudson elite racing shell. At 11.5 inches wide and 25 feet long, it's a skinny, long very "tippy" craft.

I was nervous when I pushed off, but I kept telling myself to think of all the coaching I had received through the years and all the drills I did to feel comfortable in my boat under almost any circumstance.

None of it helped right at that moment. I was nervous. Getting waked by a speed boat could fill my little shell with water, and I could end up in the lake. That was my fear.

As I rowed under the Freemont Bridge I remembered the first day I had rowed my sleek new shell. It was dark out and as a rowed down the canal, I remembered I had forgotten to log out at the boathouse. How stupid was that?

It was extremely quiet. The more I rowed, the farther I got from the boathouse, and the quieter it got. All of a sudden, my woman's intuition set in and I turned to see the gravel barge bearing down on me. I got out of the way just in the nick of time. I'll never forget the feeling of the massive barge, with a captain who couldn't even see me in my tiny shell, gliding by as I held onto my oars with everything I had, shaking with fear and cursing myself for not signing out in the log book – not that it would have even mattered.

Now, here I was again, in the same canal thinking all those thoughts when the wake hit me way above where I was afraid it would hit. Most wakes I feared were only a foot or so high. This one was much higher than that. It hit me right below my neck. I never imagined a wake could be so high. And then it was over.

Nothing bad happened. My boat only had a little water in it and I wasn't in the lake. I sat there rocking in the aftermath wondering why I didn't fall in. The drills Theresa Batty made me do probably saved me. It made me smile, and I laughed.

It's true, I thought. Ninety nine percent of the things you fear never happen. I heard a man named Dan Duke say that in 1988, and it has stuck with me all these years.

I thought of my own personal chicken and what my chicken would say to me.
The monster is never under your bed, the boogie man isn't in the closet, and the wake you think will toss you into the lake doesn't. You might as well get in your boat and row - because even if some of the things you fear do happen, they may not be even half as bad as you think.

What would your chicken say to you?

About the Authors

Marilyn Krichko

In 1998 Marilyn founded The OARS Program team building company (now Criterion Consulting Solutions). During the next decade she developed The Rowers' Code™, which is the foundation for all of their team building programs today. Marilyn is the author of *The Rowers' Code: A Business Parable of How to Pull Together as a Team - and Win*. Her business experience includes responsibility for worldwide strategy and marketing programs, IT solution's delivery, process improvement and executive/team development - working both in the USA and abroad in intense multilingual, multinational environments, requiring extensive teamwork and collaboration. Marilyn received her undergraduate degree in marketing and MBA from the University of North Florida in Jacksonville, Florida and has a certificate in Total Quality Management from Chalmers University of Technology in Sweden. When she is not at work as a corporate consultant, Marilyn is an avid rower and cyclist. She resides with her family in Seattle, WA.

Jane Rollinson

In 2006 Jane began leading the team at Criterion Consulting Solutions as President & CEO. Jane is a visible leader within the healthcare industry. She has selected and led successful teams at the local, regional, national and international levels with organizations such as Price Waterhouse, Humana, United Healthcare and Blue Cross Blue Shield. Jane has spent 30 years building and leading at the operational, executive and board levels. Jane focuses on Strategic Planning and the execution of strategies that help organizations attain profitable growth. Jane received her B.S., Business Administration from West Virginia University and advanced certificates from the Wharton School, Harvard University, the Cambridge Center for behavioral Studies and the Kellogg Graduate School at Northwestern University. Jane is an avid golfer and resides with her family in Ponte Vedra Beach, FL.

Read the Book!

The Rower's Code: A Business Parable How to Pull Together as a Team – and Win! dramatically portrays one company's experience in an intensive rowing workshop and presents a simple, actionable set of truths about teamwork and communication that can be applied to every workplace scenario to supercharge performance:

- Tap into the strength of peers
- Stay in sync with others!
- Work issues out directly with teammates!
- Personalize and powerfully leverage change!
- Unleash the effectiveness of the workgroup!
- Succeed in an increasingly competitive landscape!

Based on an overwhelming response to more than a decade of successful workshops, this book brings to life and underscores the authors' unique perspective on organizational team-building, drawing on proven, real-world results.

Published by Career Press
Hardcover: 224 pages
$19.99
ISBN: 1601631650
Available online and at book stores!

8156582R0

Made in the USA
Charleston, SC
13 May 2011